3-01

LIFE VIEWS

Published by Creative Education
123 South Broad Street, Mankato, Minnesota 56001
Creative Education is an imprint of The Creative Company

Art direction by Rita Marshall; Production design by The Design Lab/Kathy Petelinsek
Photographs by David Liebman
Additional photographs by Tom Stack & Associates (6-7)

Library of Congress Cataloging-in-Publication Data

Halfmann, Janet. Life in a tree / by Janet Halfmann; p. cm. — (LifeViews) Includes index
Summary: Examines some of the tiny and microscopic creatures who make their homes in trees,
such as bees, bark beetles, and fungi. Suggests several related activities.
ISBN 1-58341-077-5
1. Forest animals—Juvenile literature. 2. Forest ecology—Juvenile literature. 3. Trees ecology—Juvenile
literature. [1. Forest ecology. 2. Trees ecology. 3. Ecology.] I. Title. II. Series: LifeViews (Mankato, Minn.)
QL112.H34   2000
591.73—dc21   99-29966
First Edition

2   4   6   8   9   7   5   3   1

LIFE IN A
TREE

JANET HALFMANN
PHOTOGRAPHS BY DAVID LIEBMAN

TREES are like living skyscrapers. They teem with life, from the deepest roots to the tips of the highest leaves. Some tree dwellers live alone, others work together in communities, and some form unusual partnerships. Many tree dwellers, such as birds and squirrels, are easy to see. Others require a closer look. In the spring and summer, creatures lay eggs under leaves, on twigs, in bark crevices, and in special nests. Moths and butterflies emerge from cocoons, and fungi and mosses sprout and grow. Every tree is a fascinating **world** of its own, where animals survive by nibbling on leaves, digging tunnels, drinking sweet sap, and snaring prey.

Forests include a variety of trees, shrubs, and mosses.

Trees can be found nearly everywhere: in backyards, along city streets, and in forests around the world. In spring, they become home to many nest-builders. One builder is a **wasp** named the baldfaced hornet. The job of constructing the paper wasp nest falls to the queen—the only one to have survived through the winter. She is the mother of the **colony**. The hornet queen spends a few days drinking nectar before she decides on a tree for her nest. She finds a dead branch near the chosen tree and scrapes off bits of wood with her sharp jaws. She chews the wood until it's soft, then uses the paste to build her nest. After a week, the gray nest is the size of a golf ball with half a dozen six-sided rooms opening at the bottom.

The queen cements a tiny white **egg** inside each room, then fiercely guards her nest from enemies, which include spiders and birds. In a week, the eggs hatch into white larvae. The queen feeds them chewed-up caterpillars and insects. After two weeks, the offspring spin silk caps over their rooms and silk coverings, called **cocoons**, around themselves. They are now

Hornets make their nests from chewed-up wood and plant fiber. Nests are usually built in trees or attached to buildings. When finished, a nest may be larger than a basketball and contain hundreds of hornets.

pupae, a resting stage in which their bodies will completely change. This change of form is called metamorphosis and is common in the insect world. When the change is complete, the young hornets chew through the silk caps.

The newly developed hornets, all females, are called **workers**. They soon begin enlarging the nest. Now the queen's only job is to lay eggs while the workers care for her and the young. As the nest grows, it becomes pear-shaped and contains hundreds of hornets. The younger hornets work inside the nest, while older ones enlarge the nest and collect food.

On hot days, workers cool the nest by fanning their wings or by collecting water and spitting it on the outside walls. As hornets work, they watch for enemies, such as spiders and birds. Their stingers keep many enemies away, but a kind of bird called a **tanager** can snatch hornets from the air without being stung.

Toward the end of summer, some eggs develop into new queens and males called drones. They fly from the nest and

Jumping spiders (top) creep up on their prey, then pounce on it. Some species can jump more than 40 times the length of their bodies. They sometimes eat large, winged insects called cicadas (bottom).

mate. The males soon die, and the queens find a safe, warm place to spend the winter.

Another colony-builder is the **honey bee**. Honey bees build their homes in tree hollows and, unlike hornets, stay in their nests all year. All male bees die when winter comes, but the queen and female worker bees cluster together in the hive eating stored food and keeping warm.

The **queen** is the largest bee in the colony. She can live up to five years, doing nothing but laying eggs—up to 2,000 a day. She places each dot-sized egg in a wax cell, part of the **honeycomb**, and in three days it hatches into a white, worm-like larva. The workers feed the larvae royal jelly—a special food that they make—and a mixture of honey and pollen called bee bread. After six days, the larvae are full grown and become pupae. The workers seal the cells to keep the pupae safe as they change into adults. In two weeks, the new honey bees chew the lids off their cells and start their lives as workers. A **hive** contains about 80,000 workers; each lives only about five weeks.

Some types of bats live in trees, hanging from branches to sleep during the day. At night, they leave the trees to feed. In one night, a single bat may eat up to half its own body weight in flying insects.

The youngest workers keep the hive clean and take care of the larvae and the queen. Older bees go out to gather food. Flower dust, called **pollen**, sticks to the hairs on their bodies, and tiny brushes comb it into baskets on their hind legs. They sip nectar with a long, straw-like tongue and store it in a special stomach. When a honey bee has a full load, it flies back to the hive. Workers there help put the food into wax cells. Then they fan their wings over the nectar to evaporate the water, turning it into **honey**.

Returning bees dance on the honeycomb to tell their nest mates the location of the best flowers. If a bee **dances** in a circle, the flowers are close by. If it runs in a figure eight and shakes, the flowers are far away. Honey bees also use their eyes and antennae to find flowers.

When a hive becomes crowded or the queen gets old, she lays eggs that develop into new queens and males. The first new queen to emerge kills any other new queens. She flies from the hive to mate with **drones** from nearby hives. The old queen then leaves with a swarm of workers to start a new hive, while

Honey bee swarms may cover an entire tree trunk.

the new queen takes over egg-laying in her home hive. The males die after mating.

Many kinds of **caterpillars** also live in trees. Caterpillars are the young of butterflies and moths. Their bodies are soft and round. They can be fuzzy, spiny, bumpy, or smooth. All summer, caterpillars do almost nothing but eat. To spend the winter as pupae, some caterpillars build protective coverings. A moth caterpillar spins a silk cocoon, and a butterfly caterpillar forms a hard case called a **chrysalis**.

With a wingspan of almost six inches (15 cm), the Cecropia moth is the largest moth in North America. It is brown with red and white markings. Two large fake eyespots on its wings help the moth fool enemies into thinking it is a large animal.

Moths and butterflies can eat only liquids. A long, hollow feeding tube, called a **proboscis**, is used like a straw to consume nectar, tree sap, and other fluids. Some, such as the **giant silk moth**, have no mouthparts and can't eat at all. The silk moth lives on stored fat.

Many butterflies and their larvae (caterpillars) are poisonous to eat. This helps protect them from enemies. Some species, such as the tiger swallowtail (top), also have spots that look like eyes to frighten predators away.

Silk moth eggs, laid on tree leaves, hatch in about 10 days. Newly hatched caterpillars are so tiny they can barely be seen, yet some grow to be seven inches (18 cm) long. Caterpillars don't see well and depend mostly on their **antennae** to find their way around. They have six strong, fat legs. In addition, leg-like walking stubs, called **prolegs**, have tiny hooks that the caterpillar uses to climb on stems and leaves.

Caterpillars are a favorite food of songbirds and many other animals, so many hide by blending in with their surroundings. This is called **camouflage**. An example of camouflage is the inchworm, or looper. Gripping a surface with only its hind legs, it can pose like a straight green twig for hours.

Butterfly caterpillars that form their chrysalises in trees include many of the **swallowtails**. To become a pupa, the swallowtail caterpillar first spins a little silk platform to hold onto with the hooks on its hind legs. Then it spins a silk safety belt to hold the top of its body to a branch. Next, it sheds its skin, and a hard-shelled chrysalis forms around its body. Near the end of the pupal stage, the form of the adult is vis-

Some kinds of skinks (top), a type of small lizard, live in trees. They eat mostly insects and other small creatures, including centipedes, and may eat worms as well when they descend to the ground.

Arthur Miller

Arthur Miller (born 1915) has always exhibited winning form. As an undergraduate at Michigan, his plays won university awards. His first Broadway play, **The Man Who Had All the Luck** (1944), closed after four shows, but set in motion his examination of the faltering father-son relationship. This theme provided the bedrock for **Death of a Salesman** (1949), which won the Pulitzer Prize for drama. Those attending the 1999 New York production starring Brian Dennehy would attest that the interplay between Willy Loman and his sons Biff and Happy still captures and wrenches even 50 years later.

Miller also wrote **All My Sons** (1947), **The Crucible** (1953), and the screenplay for **The Misfits** (1961).

ible through the chrysalis. At last the shell splits, and the butterfly slowly emerges.

Swallowtails are among the largest and prettiest of the butterflies. They get their name from the "tails" hanging down from their wings, which resemble the wings of a swallow.

Despite their name, **box elder** bugs don't live exclusively on box elder trees. These black bugs with red markings are about one-half inch (1.3 cm) long. They have a sharp beak that pierces seeds, leaves, and twigs. The beak acts like a straw, drawing up food juices.

Another insect, the **bark beetle**, lives most of its life under tree bark. One of a pair of beetles bores through the bark and makes a small room. The partner follows, and the two mate. The female then chews a long channel just under the bark. Along each side of the channel are a series of tiny pockets into which she lays an egg. When the tiny, white **larvae** hatch, they dig tunnels out from the main channel as they eat their way through the wood. The pattern they create looks like a centipede with lots of long legs. The larvae spend the winter in

Some beetles use powerful jaws called mandibles to chew on trees. Many beetles are pests that feed on farm crops and trees, but others—such as ladybugs—help humans by eating other insect pests.

these tunnels. In the spring they become pupae, then emerge as adults, each about the size of a grain of rice. The only time bark beetles spend outside the tree is when the adults fly to other trees to find mates.

While most bark beetles don't kill trees, the European elm bark beetle is dangerous because it carries a **fungus** that causes Dutch elm disease. This disease has killed millions of elm trees in America and Europe by blocking the tubes inside the trunk that carry water throughout the tree.

Fungi belong to a kingdom separate from plants because, unlike plants, they do not have the ability to make their own food. Instead, fungi get their food from living or dead plants or animals. The body of a fungus is made up of thousands of fine threads that form a tangled **web** inside a tree or under the ground. Many fungi also make a fruiting body, like the familiar mushroom. This is the part that is visible on the outside of the tree or above the ground.

Fungi that feed on a living tree are called **parasites**

Fungi come in many shapes and sizes. Some are parasites that grow on trees by taking the nutrients that the tree needs to live. Common types of fungi include mushrooms and bracket fungi.

because they hurt the tree, usually causing the wood to rot. A common tree parasite is bracket fungus. It looks like hard, leathery shelves and appears in many shades of brown or orange.

Not all fungi that make their homes on trees are parasites, though. Some fungi team with algae to form **lichens**. The algae supply the food, and the fungi keep the algae moist and attach the lichen to the tree. Such teamwork is called **symbiosis** and is common in the animal and plant worlds.

The 25,000 species of lichens look like flat crusts, bunches of leaves, or little bushes. They can be yellow, green, or gray. Their colors are brighter after a rainfall because the **algae** show through the water-filled fungus threads. Lichens that grow on trees in North America include lung lichen, cracked shield lichen, and beard lichen. Insects and caterpillars feed on lichens, and **hummingbirds** and other birds use them to cover and camouflage their nests.

Fungi also team up with the **roots** of certain trees. The tree provides food for the fungi, and the fungi transfer water and minerals from the soil to the tree. Often, one couldn't survive

Many types of lizards and frogs are at home in trees. These include anoles (top and left), spring peepers (middle), and tree lizards (right). These creatures all have unique toes that make them excellent climbers.

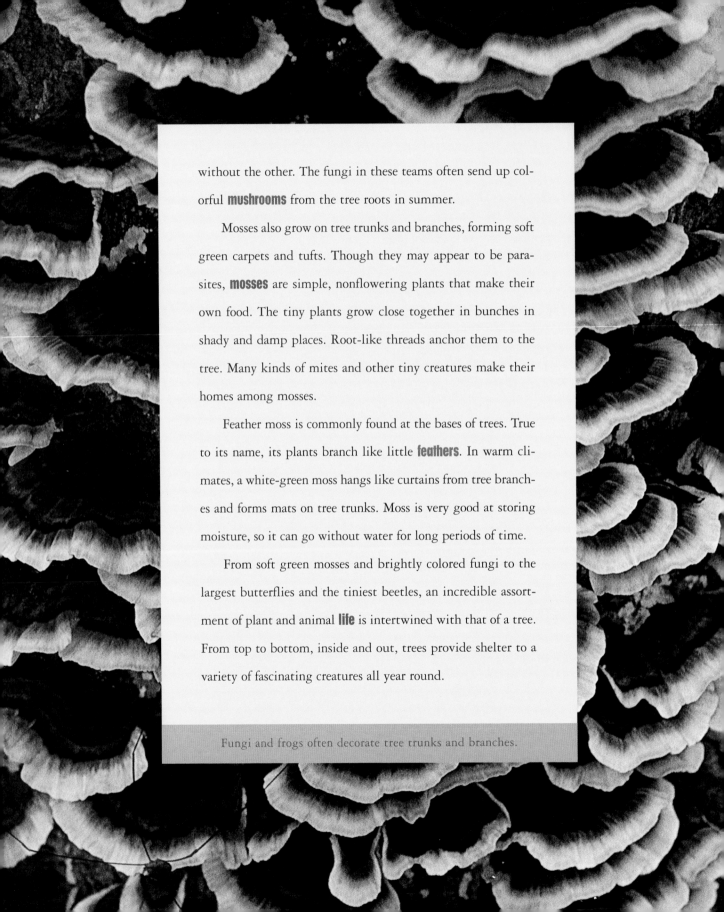

without the other. The fungi in these teams often send up colorful **mushrooms** from the tree roots in summer.

Mosses also grow on tree trunks and branches, forming soft green carpets and tufts. Though they may appear to be parasites, **mosses** are simple, nonflowering plants that make their own food. The tiny plants grow close together in bunches in shady and damp places. Root-like threads anchor them to the tree. Many kinds of mites and other tiny creatures make their homes among mosses.

Feather moss is commonly found at the bases of trees. True to its name, its plants branch like little **feathers**. In warm climates, a white-green moss hangs like curtains from tree branches and forms mats on tree trunks. Moss is very good at storing moisture, so it can go without water for long periods of time.

From soft green mosses and brightly colored fungi to the largest butterflies and the tiniest beetles, an incredible assortment of plant and animal **life** is intertwined with that of a tree. From top to bottom, inside and out, trees provide shelter to a variety of fascinating creatures all year round.

Fungi and frogs often decorate tree trunks and branches.

RAISING CATERPILLARS

It's amazing to see a caterpillar transform into a butterfly or moth right before your eyes.

You Will Need

- Small jar and cover with holes
- Large jar, fish bowl, or aquarium and cover with holes
- Leaves and branches from caterpillar's food plant
- Sticks
- Soil or peat moss and dry leaves
- Paper towel or sponge; foil or plastic wrap
- Water spray bottle

Collecting Caterpillars

In spring and early summer, look for caterpillars on plants, shrubs, and trees. If you see partly eaten leaves, caterpillars may be nearby. Caterpillars are delicate and some have stinging hairs, so an easy way to collect one is to break off the branch it's on and put the whole thing into a small container with holes. It's important to note the kind of plant the caterpillar is on, so you'll know what to feed it. Many caterpillars are fussy and will eat only one kind of plant.

Larvae Munchers

You can keep caterpillars in a small container when they're little, but as they grow, you must put them in a bigger cage, such as a large jar, fish bowl, or aquarium. It's best to put different kinds of caterpillars in separate containers. Every day, put fresh leaves and branches from the caterpillar's food plant in the cage. You can keep the food fresh longer by wrapping a wet paper towel around the stems and covering them with foil or plastic wrap. Spray the cage lightly with water, but don't let much moisture collect on the sides. Caterpillars are messy, so you'll need to remove wastes often,

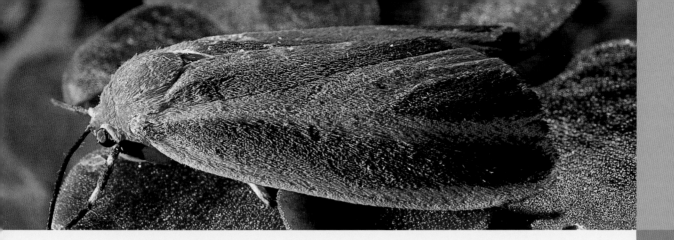

and wash and dry the container from time to time. Cover the top of the cage with an aquarium screen or mesh held by a rubber band. Set the cage in a shady place. Caterpillars shed their skin several times as they grow. This is called molting. They are fragile during this time and shouldn't be touched.

Forming Pupae

When the caterpillars become restless and stop eating, they are ready to turn into pupae, the resting stage before they emerge as butterflies or moths. Some hang from their food plants inside a cocoon or chrysalis, and others burrow into the soil or under leaves. Unless you know exactly what your caterpillar needs, provide a few upright sticks for hanging pupae, and put some moist soil or peat moss and dry leaves in the bottom of the cage. Sprinkle the leaves lightly with water. Be careful not to bother the caterpillars when they are changing into pupae.

The Big Change

Pupae that form during the spring or early summer usually complete their change in a few weeks. Provide twigs for the moth or butterfly to climb on, and make sure there's enough room for it to spread its wings. Put a moist pad of paper towel or damp sponge in the cage to create a moist environment for the insect to expand its wings properly. After the moth or butterfly emerges, wait for its wings to dry. Then release the new adult near flowers.

If a caterpillar becomes a pupa in the fall, the adult most likely won't emerge until the following spring or summer. If there are pupae in the cage when cold weather begins, put the container in a cold place, such as an unheated garage or a protected spot outdoors. When it gets warm in spring, bring the container indoors and sprinkle it lightly every day with water. After the adult emerges and its wings dry, release it to fly away.

GROW A TREE

You can see how a tree's roots, trunk, and leaves grow by sprouting your own avocado tree from a seed.

You Will Need

- Avocado pit (well-ripened fruit works best)
- Tall glass or jar
- Pot and potting soil
- Toothpicks
- Lukewarm water

What To Do

1. Peel the brown papery covering off the pit.
2. Poke three or four toothpicks around the pit's center.
3. Suspend the pit, pointed side up, over a tall glass or jar filled with lukewarm water.
4. Add water as needed to keep the bottom half of the seed covered. Change the water once a week.
5. Place the jar in a sunny window.

In three to four weeks, your avocado will sprout. When its stem and roots are a few inches long, plant it in a large pot. To get your tree to branch out, cut off the top third when your plant is about nine inches (23 cm) tall. Enjoy watching your avocado tree grow!

LEARN MORE ABOUT TREES

American Beekeeping Federation
P.O. Box 1038
Jesup, GA 31598-1038
http://www.abfnet.org/

American Bryological and
    Lichenological Society
c/o James D. Lawrey
Biology Department
George Mason University
4400 University Drive
Fairfax, VA 22030-4444
http://ucjeps.herb.berkeley.edu/bryolab/
    ABLS/about.ABLS.html

American Forest Foundation
1111 19th Street NW
Suite 780
Washington, D.C. 20036
http://www.affoundation.org

The National Arbor Day Foundation
100 Arbor Avenue
Nebraska City, NE 68410
http://www.arborday.org

North American Butterfly Association
4 Delaware Road
Morristown, NJ 07960
http://www.naba.org/

North American Mycological Association
Executive Secretary
10 Lynn Brooke Place
Charleston, WV 25312-9521
http://namyco.org/

National Honey Board
390 Lashley Street
Longmont, CO 80501-6045
http://www.nhb.org/

The Xerces Society
4828 Southeast Hawthorne Boulevard
Portland, Oregon 97215
http://www.xerces.org

INDEX

All life in a tree is interconnected.